Hypnotic Selling

Jody N Holland

DEDICATION

This book is dedicated to the people who keep the world
spinning, who keep their companies winning, the people
who sell day in and day out; they are my heroes without a
doubt!

CONTENTS

ACKNOWLEDGEMENTS

My greatest acknowledgement that I could give is the thanks that I feel to all of those who have given me the opportunity to learn, to grow, and to advance based on experience. Were it not for the failures and frustrations, I would never have been able to achieve success.

1 THE MINDSET OF A WINNER

I remember very clearly stepping into the ring with him. He was bigger than I was and we were the same rank. He had won his last three fights and he was good. He was really good. I remember thinking about his fighting style. I knew that he almost always lead with a left back fist and then followed it up with either a right reverse punch or a right round-house. His standard mode of operation was to overpower his opponent and then keep them on the run. I also knew that he had two weaknesses. First, he believed that his size would intimidate his opponent. He thought that because he had grown more than most kids in his class, he would be able to scare them. Second, he always left his ribs vulnerable when he threw his back fist. I had studied him because he had the advantage. He had a longer reach and more brute strength. I knew that he would underestimate me because I was a full foot shorter than him. I would exploit that and then taunt him. I knew that he got flustered if he was ever put on the ropes and that would be just what I did to him. He was brazen. I was clinical. I would be precise and calculated in my attack. I knew what he could do to me. I also knew what he planned to do because he attacked in almost the same way every time. I learned from observation. I learned from what he did. I learned and applied the new information before, during, and after each encounter. I would do the same here.

The referee started the match and he immediately extended his left arm and leaned slightly toward me as he shot the back of his fist toward my face. As his hand screamed through the air, I leaned back on my back foot and connected a perfect round-house kick to his solo-plexus area and followed it with a round-house to his nose without dropping my foot. I then planted my left front foot on the ground and pivoted to the inside to execute a reverse hook kick, which landed squarely on his right ear. I reversed back down and jumped straight up, landing a front snap kick under his jaw and knocking him out cold.

As he hit the mat, I stepped back to my corner and waited. The ref checked him and indicated that the fight was over. He was out and I had won. I had won because of my mind more than I had won because of my physical prowess. I was physically prepared for the fight, but I was more mentally prepared than anything. I knew my opponent. I knew what I was up against. I had done my research and I did not get cocky, like he did. I pushed myself to be ready for what he would likely throw and he did not disappoint me. I won the battle because I had the mindset of a winner.

It doesn't matter if you are on the mat or in the boardroom, it is your mindset that will set you apart from everyone else. There are five distinctive characteristics of a winning mindset. The cool part of these characteristics is that they are actually just choices about what you believe. The Belief Systems (BS) that you have in your head are what have always guided your thoughts. Your thoughts have always guided your actions. Your actions have always created your results. And your results have always created the experience that you have in this life. If you want to have a winning mindset, you start with the right beliefs.

My BS

The first characteristic of a winning mindset is the **Old-Dog-New-Tricks** characteristic. Many of us have heard the saying, "You can't teach an old dog new tricks." I say that is losing BS. Winning BS is what we learn every single day. We learn new tricks in each moment of life, if we are paying attention and we want to learn. A winner believes that learning and growing are part of who they are. There is never an age that we reach where learning is no longer a possibility. It is always possible. In fact, learning is habitual. If you are a morning person, it is ideal to wake up and study for 30 minutes in the morning. If you are a night person, shift to the evening. Find four seminars a year to go to that interest you and offer you a chance to grow in an area that is important to you. I go to seminars on business, accounting, writing, personal development, sales, and more. You can grow as often as you would like, but you have to do something new in order to master your world at a higher level. Doing what you have always done will simply get you what you have always gotten. Because you are a winner, you know that all dogs learn new tricks. You know that you can learn by simply observing what is going on around you. Even if you are not off at a seminar, you can pick up new ways of leading, selling, or even just connecting. You are a winner because you know that you are always learning and applying new information. In Paulo Cuello's book, The Alchemist, Santiago learns how the camels interact with the desert and how the desert interacts with the wind. He learns that there is a language that can be understood by anyone because it is a universal language and it has nothing to do with words. Santiago learned because Santiago wanted to learn. You learn because you believe that there is value in learning and because you are a winner.

The second characteristic of a winning mindset is the **One In The Same** characteristic. Too many people walk around believing that they are not connected to and influencing those around them. They see the things that are happening around them as unrelated and therefore miss the connection between one event and another. The simple reality is that every interaction that you have with another person will either leave them better off or worse off. We are all connected at a root level. Scientists have been able to show that saying nice things to a plant will actually make it grow faster and stronger. Saying mean things to a plant will stunt its growth. I know that I am even more receptive to the things around me than the average sweet potato. Knowing this, I work hard to surround myself with positive and uplifting things. I also realize that my attitude and mental state will impact the person that I am presenting to. I need to keep the right focus in order to get the right response. Zig Ziglar used to tell salespeople that the customer would only buy your product if you believed in it enough to buy it first. If you are selling Toyotas, then you should drive a Toyota. If you sell nutrition products, then you should use them yourself. People will naturally believe in a believer. They will naturally doubt a doubter. We are all a part of the same Cosmos. The second side of this is that you will tend to get what you wish for others. If you wish only good for others, then you will get more good in your own life. If you hate rich people, then you will never be able to be one. Wealth will stay outside of your grasp. If you want to be a rich and successful person, then you must respect them and learn from them. If you want to be respected, then you must give respect. Embody the result that you wish to achieve and the result will find you. Everything is connected!

The third characteristic of a winning mindset is the **You Are Not Your Khaki's** characteristic. You are connected to everything around you, but you are not defined by those things. One of the things that Tyler Derden says in "Fight Club" is that people are not defined by their things. Being successful and happy is the choice that you make. It isn't something that you earn. If you are the type of salesperson that is always comparing yourself to some other, more successful person then you will find that you have trouble getting there. Comparison kills your joy and steals your thunder. It robs you of your chance to live in the moment, without fear, without reservation, and full of life. Since people are buying you before they buy your product or service, it is important that you are genuine. You are not your car, your house, your watch, your shoes, or any other combination of your stuff. You are you. When you can become comfortable in your skin, you will become confident in your pursuits. Don't try to be anyone but yourself. The objective is to simply live as the highest version of yourself. Live in such a way that the world feels automatically connected to you. When a person is confident in who they are, the world responds. There is an energy that surrounds that level of confidence. You are not your Khakis!

The fourth characteristic of a winning mindset is the **Kaizen** characteristic. Kaizen is a Japanese term based of the philosophy of Dr. Edwards Deming. Deming believed in continuous and never-ending improvement. He used this philosophy in business, particularly in manufacturing, to help people look for one way to improve today over yesterday. In sales, this philosophy is incredible for advancing your success. Early on in my sales career, we referred to this as the "one more" concept. Nike has done a great job of capitalizing on the "And 1®" concept. At the end of the day, make one more call. At the end of your day, try one more time to connect with someone. If you will find a way to improve your results, not your efforts, by 1% over yesterday, you will grow without ceasing. You will improve every aspect of who you are in sales and your results will show. Too many people live the opposite direction and think that they will do less and focus less on results and somehow the money will show up magically in their account. Throughout this book, you will be learning the concept of results improvement. The objective of this book is to teach you how to improve your results by connecting better, presenting better, closing better, and delivering better than you did in the past. What can you do today to improve your results over yesterday?

The fifth characteristic of a winning mindset is the **Einstein** characteristic. The Einstein characteristic says that the world is full of wonderment and learning opportunities. Einstein once said, "I want to know the thoughts of God. The rest are details." His outlook on research was one of being excited everyday for the opportunity to solve one more challenge. He was thankful for his challenges, not frustrated by them. He loved a good puzzle and couldn't wait to find out how the pieces fit together. Sales is a game. It can be seen as chess or a puzzle, or whatever kind of game fits your personality. The simple reality is that you are waking up every day and looking for ways to play the game better, to have more fun while doing so, and to achieve greater results. Wake up excited for the opportunity to see who else you can help through the products and services that you offer. Having a winning mindset means finding where the pieces fit and looking forward to that challenge each and every day.

Your mindset is the foundation of your sales

success. When your mindset is that of a winner, you win. There are three things that I want you to do in order to be wildly successful from this chapter. I know what you are thinking already, "Is this gonna be hoaky?" I want to assure you of one thing. The people who are willing to do these exercises are the ones that make the most money and help the most customers/clients. If you are telling yourself that you are too cool to be successful, then you may very well spend your life being cool and broke. I would encourage you to test me on these exercises. Take a close look at what your belief system is about you. I don't and can't know you like you know you. I don't know what your BS (belief system) is right now. What I do know is that you will not believe the things that I tell you as much as you will believe the things that you tell you. I have never disagreed with anything that I believed. In fact, you have always agreed with the things that you believed as well. We have that in common! If I tell you something it means one thing. If you tell yourself the same thing, it means everything. So, here are your exercises to solidify your winning mindset.

Exercise 1: I will wake up every day and start with a smile and a happy body. Your physiology (posture, facial expressions, etc) is in control of your emotions. When you wake up, I want you to smile for 5 minutes and walk around looking like you are a happy person. If you will choose to do this, you will set the tone for your day and change the energy around you.

Exercise 2: I will tell myself what I am doing

right to get to where I am going at least 3 times per day. Write down the five or fewer things that must be done every day in order for you to be successful. In sales, these are generally to connect with people, tell your story, ask for the business, and deliver the goods. You may have different ones, but what ever they are, you need to say out loud that you are doing those things every day and that is why success is all over you!

Exercise 3: I will learn something new today. Every day, you have to learn something new. You have to learn a new word, a new technique for sales, a new way of connecting, or anything else new that you would like to focus on. Learning something new every day sets you apart from the vast majority of the world. Winners are learners and you learn because you are a winner!

2 PEOPLE PLAY OUTSIDE

People play outside of themselves when they face a problem. When you can keep this in mind in your interactions with prospects and customers, you significantly enhance your odds of winning. They are looking for a solution and you are one option for finding that solution. Think about the last time that you had a challenge in business. If you think about it, really think about it, you could likely admit that you knew the right answer, even when you asked others what you should do. The simple reality is that most of us want a second opinion on the choices that we need to make at work. This seems to be particularly true for people who are facing choices that will affect the course of their business, or when they are dealing with things that they have not done well at in the past.

The statement of "If you knew what to do, you would already be doing it" isn't actually true. The reality is that most of us know what to do, we just don't choose to do it. We have a tendency to explain the bad things or the tough things in our lives as external to our control. This explanation lends itself to those who desire to be hypnotic in their selling. It sets you up for being able to strongly influence others by using structured messaging. This isn't trickery, it is good strategy for helping the client identify the things that they believe are out of their control and that they will need help with. These are the things that make the difference between "Nice product" and "I have to have that." Our objective is to get the prospect to convince us that they should buy from us.

This inverted perspective on sales takes all of the actual pressure off of you, the salesperson. It sets things up to allow people to realize that they need you and to pursue an engagement with you. It also positions you to operate on your own terms. You don't have to cave to crazy demands because it isn't you that is trying to convince them. It is they who are trying to convince you. Just to make sure this is sinking in, understanding that people play outside, or look for answers to their problems outside of themselves, this means that you are the one in front of them. If you ask them the right question set and listen effectively, they will tell you exactly what challenge they are facing, what isn't working for them, and what they want to buy from you. You will have the opportunity to serve the clients that you want by uncovering these three specifics.

1. W.I.N. – The first and perhaps most important thing to understand from any potential client is what's important now?

Each person will have an area that is important to them. This is what you are looking for, not what their problem is, but what their focus is. The big mistake that we tend to make in selling is that we want to uncover problems. We want to expose that pain right up front and then pour a little salt on the wound or twist the knife, or whatever analogy you want to use. The point is that people become defensive when you go straight for the attack. You have to go for the WIN, not the kill. Understanding what is important to the client… related to what you offer is what sets you apart from others. One of the tactics that can make this easy is to outline in a graphic or info-graphic the areas that you serve the client. Please note that I did not say what products you have to offer. I said to look at your areas of service. See the example below of what my graphic representation looks like.

F.I.R.S.T.E.P. 2 Success Program
What's Important Now?

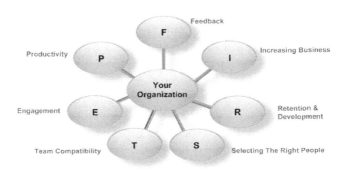

2. The second thing you want to look at is why
   that service area is important to them.
   During this phase, you are uncovering their
   reasoning behind the importance of that
   given area. It is the reason why that creates
   emotional attachment to the outcome. If
   you can't get them to talk about why the
   area is important, it is unlikely you will get
   them to desire to move forward with you.
   In order to stack the deck in your favor,
   you will want to be strategic about your
   questions here as well. First, make sure
   that you ask directly, "Why is that area
   important to you and/or your business?"
   Don't dance around the topic, just ask.
   When they start talking about the
   importance, you will want to listen very
   carefully to what they say and how they say
   it. You are looking for subtle nuances in

their facial expressions, sometimes referred to as micro-expressions. These micro-expressions are things like an eye-twitch or a deep breath in before they answer or looking up and away before answering the question. You will learn these things more in-depth in a later chapter. Suffice it to say, they are important. Next, you want to focus on what it means to them if they accomplished this objective and did it within a specified timeframe. I will typically ask, "What would it mean to you and/or your business if I were able to come in and make you successful in this particular priority in the next 60 days?" My objective is to plant in their mind the idea of making them successful at this in the next 60 days. I want them to see me helping them in their mind. I want them to associate good thoughts with the progress. That is what creates the positive emotional attachment to me and to my services that will make it easier for them to play in my court with the third step. Building up this positive emotional energy puts me on the same team as them and positions in their mind the idea that I am here to help them.

3. The third thing that you need to find out is how they are moving things forward. Please note that the vast majority of people that I have presented to over the last decade and a half of professional selling have no idea how they are making things

better. They don't know because they typically are not doing anything to make it better. This is the pain part for them. It is just that most people have not discussed what is most important to them and then had to relay what they were actually doing about it. When they talk through what they are doing, it is generally at that moment that they realize that they aren't really doing anything to make things better. They have been able to avoid it in the past, though, because they have indicated that it was important and then stopped the conversation. Your job is to move that conversation forward. Once they open up about the fact that they are not getting the results that they desire, then you ask them about the "now" part. The truth is that nobody really likes to admit that they aren't moving things forward. Because of this, be sure to craft your question in a positive light, one that doesn't make them look bad. For example, you would ask, "Based on what you said, selecting the right people is important to you and would likely help solve several of your business challenges. You indicated that your current solution is not getting you all of the results that you need. Would you be interested in looking at a solution that would meet the rest of your needs in that area?" What you are doing is reiterating what they said and then asking them if they want to move things forward. You are NOT telling them that they are screwing up, or that they desperately need you, or anything arrogant. You are simply there as an observer and facilitator and your singular desire is to help them achieve their goals.

The W.I.N. perspective is one that will set you apart from most other sales reps. Look at the best that exists in others. Don't judge their past decisions. Remember, people make the best decisions that they can with the information that they have. Once they have further evaluated their situation, you are able to help them make a new decision with new information.

3 GOOD VIBRATIONS

In looking at the quantum physics of reality, Deepak Chopra explains that matter isn't matter at all. An atom, once considered the fundamental building block of matter as we know it, has 3 component parts. Each of the parts of an atom (proton, neutron, and electron) have their fundamental parts. When you go down as far as you can, you end up with only trace energy. This energy is what makes up all things that make up all things. If all things are made up of the same fundamental energy, then that means that all things are truly connected.

Taking it from a different angle, the conscious mind and the subconscious mind work together to ensure that a person can process all the right information. The conscious mind deals with the outer world and determines what gets through the filter to the subconscious. The job of the conscious mind is to filter. It will delete, distort, and generalize the things that are thrown at it until they are neatly organized and manageable. The tough part of this is that the conscious mind runs off of programming that we have developed over the years. If you have consistently interpreted events as attacks on you and believe that you deserve to be attacked, then you will consistently get attacked.

Whether you wish to look at it from a quantum physics perspective or a psychological perspective, the simple reality remains true. It is the unseen that attracts, builds, and creates the seen. It is the vibrational energy, fundamental energy, that makes up actual reality. This means that it is critical to understand what vibrational energy you are operating at. You have to look at your life and the view that you hold of reality.

I knew a guy once that believed that bad things just happened to him. He looked for those bad things and, you guessed it, he found them. I worked hard to convince him to dream of what the possibilities could be. He spent one day looking at houses he would like to buy and land he would like to buy, and then had a letter from the IRS waiting on him when he got home. He proceeded to cuss at me for encouraging him to look for good. If you spend your life trying to attract junk into your life, it may not reverse the second that you try a better thought pattern. It may take a while to get you there. The sad truth for this guy is that his mind is creating his reality. The part that is sad is that he could create any reality that he wanted.

John Milton, in <u>Paradise Lost</u> said, "The mind is

its own place, and in itself can make a heaven of hell, a hell of heaven." I took this to mean that we can make something great out of our circumstance or we can make something awful out of it. Your focus is what will attract the same vibrational energy. It will literally make your world. People who are consistently lucky seem to look for and expect luck. People who are consistently unlucky seem to look for and expect bad luck.

Your vibrational energy is transmitted to the world around you. It doesn't matter if you mean to transmit it or not. What matters is if you can focus on transmitting good and raising your frequency. Think about what a truly happy person who is also very successful looks like. Do they look hunched over, with a frown on their face, and with their brow furrowed? NO! They stand tall, shoulders back, a smile slightly curled at all times on their face, walking with confidence to their destination. That is what a happy and successful person looks like!

So, what do you look like? Do you walk around with disdain for your lot in life plastered about you? Or, do you walk around with hope and fire and drive and joy exuding from your every pore? The part that most people have trouble wrapping their mind around is the fact that it is simply a choice. It is simply a choice as to which direction you face when facing the world. The choice is not a one-time event though. The choice is something that must be made every single day. You must choose to face your day with joy and hope and confidence, every day and sometimes several times during the day. You must focus continuously on being the kind of person that others would love to be.

There are three reasons that this is important. Each has its own merit and each supports the others.

1. You are happier when you choose to see the good and vibrate at that level. If for no other reason than enjoying your time on this planet, choosing to give off that happy vibe is much more enjoyable than trying to get others to see you suffer. Suffering isn't near as fun as the brochure makes it out to be.

2. Others want to be like happy and successful people. You will attract the kind of people to you that match your vibration. If you want to attract angry and unhappy people, just be angry and unhappy. If you want to attract happy and successful people, then be happy and successful. Whether you are talking about clients or personal relationships, it is your focus that draws like-minded individuals to you.

3. People buy you before they buy your product or service. Given the choice between doing business with a happy person or an unhappy person, I will always choose the happy one. It isn't that I am prejudice against the joy-avoiders. It is just that I am preferential to the joy-expanders. You will find in your persuasion career that it is your attitude that truly determines the altitude of your

success and the latitude of your forgiveness from others.

Walk in life with good vibrations, and good vibrations will surround you. A few things that will help you achieve this are listed here.

1. Make the first thing out of your mouth in the morning something positive. When your alarm goes off, if you use an alarm, say something like, "Today is going to be awesome and I am ready for my blessings." A few other ideas for the starting phrase for the day are… "Life is great and today it will be even better!" "I am stoked about today!" "Today, I choose joy and success will beat down the door to join me."

2. Be grateful for what you have. I have never met a successful person who had plenty that wasn't first grateful for all that he had. Even if you are living on the street in a cardboard box, be thankful for your box. You can think of something to be grateful for every day. Be grateful to be alive, to be moving, to have opportunity, to be reading a book, to simply be.

3. Practice random acts of kindness and senseless acts of beauty. I have found that my good vibrations go up instantly when I do something good for others without expecting

anything in return. I might pay for someone's food behind me in the drive-thru line. A friend of my wife's will tape Ziploc snack bags with $2 in them around the Dollar Store with a note that says, "You have just experienced a random act of kindness. Pass it on." I have taken food to people who needed it and snuck away without being noticed. That one takes some serious ninja skills, but it sure is fun. I have picked up trash in a park for no other reason than to make it look better. Whatever you decide to do, make the world and others a little better.

You are a reflection of your thoughts. You must feed good stuff into your brain, filter out the bad stuff, and intentionally be awesome! It is your inner awesomeness that makes your outer awesomeness.

4 YIN-YANG AND A CHICKEN WING

There is a balance to this life. It isn't just a balance between good and evil, though. It is a balance between duality and potentiality. Think about what the potential is that exists within you. Do you have the potential to take action and accomplish something great? Do you have the potential to do nothing and accomplish nothing? Do you have the potential to change the world for the better? Do you have the potential to change the world for the worse? Every encounter that you have with a prospect represents a duality of potential outcomes.

Each side of the duality has the seeds of the opposite side embedded within it. For example, when a prospect is not agreeing with you, they still have the potential to change their minds and want to buy everything that you have, and then some. On the other side, a customer who has already bought has the potential to stop using your products or services. The potential is always there. It is simply waiting for you to tap into it and make something of it. Potential isn't results, however. The potential that exists is only potential until something energizes it and gives it momentum. I have always said that people buy what you're selling when what you're selling solves their problems and they know it. You can have the greatest potential in the world, but it will remain only potential until you take action.

The meaning of the Chines Yin-Yang Symbol expands the concept of duality and potentiality. The Chinese believe that everything is made up of energy and potential. Each thing has the potential to be good and the potential to be bad. Each person has the potential for success and the potential for failure. If you look at the symbol, it is a black swirl with a white dot and a white swirl with a black dot. The black swirl is the Yang and contains the seeds of the Yin. The white swirl is the Yin and contains the seeds of the Yang. They are positioned as if they are swirling, indicating that both have equal power without focus. It is your focus that gives greater energy to one or the other.

From a sales standpoint, there are lots of people in this world that try to sell things based on the fear and darkness. Insurance salespeople are the first to pop into my mind. I can hear the rep now saying, "You don't want to leave your family without anything and probably living on the streets because you didn't buy this policy, do you?" I've never met a mobster, but I would imagine they would use the same kind of offer. They are trying to push, without balancing out the needs of the person. There is a Yin and a Yang to the interaction. It is critical that we push people to reveal what is important and why and then receive their information and their purchase. To me, it is the difference between trying to hard-close and simply allowing the person to buy.

The origin of JuiJitsu came from a monk meditating and watching the falling snow. He watched as the snow fell to the branches and slowly piled up, pressing down on the branch. The weight of the snow continued to mount until the branch yielded and allowed the snow to complete its course to the ground. The monk wondered which had won. Had the branch defeated the snow or had the snow defeated the branch? The snow had led the attack, but the branch had used the weight of the snow against itself, sending it on its way and then recovering to where the branch was originally. It was in yielding that victory was attained, concluded the monk. The same is true in hypnotic selling. It is in yielding to what the prospect desires that we redirect the prospect to make a purchase. They would not have been talking with you if they weren't already on that pathway. This means that it is their intended path to solve their issues and it is your role to yield with the right solution.

This goes beyond the simple interaction with the prospect. This goes into your philosophy of life. Are you the kind of person who is willing to give up your time and expertise and likely your ego in order to create action? Are you the type of person who is willing to receive the blessings that are given to you as a result of your action? Do you believe that the seeds of blessing reside in the swirl of action? So how does it all begin? The Yang starts an action and the Yin receives it. Just like this, you have to be willing to both demonstrate action and receive blessing. The mistake that many people make is that they want to receive blessing but never give right action. Others take massive action but don't believe in the blessing. The two sides have to work in harmony with one another. After all, each side contains the seed of its reflection.

When you get caught up in the stress of selling, you can easily forget that it isn't real. I don't mean that it isn't real in a "The Matrix Has You" sort of way. What I mean is that everything is potential. Nothing is real until it is done. So, why not enjoy the game of creation? I have practiced this hundreds of times in my life. When I am approaching a rental counter to pick up my car, I think… "What would make them want to give me a free upgrade?" I then proceed to connect with the person behind the counter and engage them in conversation. I make them laugh and I throw out that I am currently available to be upgraded for free. I usually get it. I have even played the game to get a free chicken wing at a restaurant. It is just fun to see if people will bless you when you ask. I have actually gotten free meals, free drinks, extra food, hotel upgrades, rental car upgrades, contract extensions, discounts on clothes, and a free trip because I was playing the game.

Pick your favorite game. Whether it is Monopoly®, or Chess, or Beer Pong, it doesn't matter. Just pick your game. Now think about your strategy to win the game and what happens if you lose the game. The simple truth is that if you lose the game, you learn a lesson and just play another game. The first time I lost at Monopoly®, which was the first time that I played, I learned a lot. I wasn't stressed about all of my moves. I was relaxed and having fun. Hypnotic selling is the same thing. It is a game that is lots of fun. It is fun to see what you can generate in the way of Yin, blessings. What is it that you are willing to receive if someone is willing to give it. Do you turn down simple compliments? Do you tell people that you aren't special when they try to compliment you? Stop it if you are doing that. Accept their blessing. Simply say, "Thank you."

Chicken Wings

Let's play a game. I want you to take some action in this chapter. I want you to see if you can convince someone to give you something for free or for a reduced price. You will need to have just a couple of elements included in the request to make it work. Here is an example…

I <u>wanted</u> to see if you would <u>give</u> me an extra pickle with my sandwich <u>because</u> I love pickles and you would make me very <u>happy</u> if you did.

You are telling them that you want something. They would have to give it to you, meaning they have the power. You use the flow of words like I did in order to create mental justification. You let them have power again by indicating that your happiness depends on it. The entire time that you are talking to them, position your body posture with confidence and smile at them. You can even try to be a little funny if you want, but you have to smile!

This game is an absolute blast and I play it as often as I can. The really cool thing about the chicken wing game is that it makes others happy to make you happy. In reality, they are winning as big as you are. You may get a free chicken wing, but they get a big smile and a funny story.

Once you play the game, I want to hear about it. Go to www.jodyholland.com and send me a message. Or, you can email me at jody@jodyholland.com. I would love to hear about what you get for free.

Keep in mind that this might take multiple attempts to get it right. It does work if you follow the simple rules and you will get your chicken wings. Just like any other game that you have learned to play, it takes practice. I practice regularly and have more fun playing the game all the time.

Phase II of this is to see selling and business itself as a game. You will find that approaching others with the attitude of seeing if you can get a free chicken wing makes it a lot easier to ask for $50,000 contract. If you get it, you get it and it will be awesome. If you don't get it, you don't get it and you will learn from the game and go to the next one.

DO THE CHICKEN WING EXERCISE NOW

Chicken Wing Notes

_____

_____

_____

_____

_____

_____

_____

_____

_____

_____

_____

_____

5 SOCRATES WAS RIGHT

Socrates taught that all knowledge exists within man. He meant that everything that you would need to know is available by asking the right set of questions. Think about the way that you go into a sales presentation. The old school model would be to go in and tout how incredible your company is and what great products you have, and how 9 out of 10 people prefer doing business with you. This model is one that pushes information on the prospect and tries to overwhelm them with the reasons that they made a bad decision in the past. This is contrary to the Hypnotic Selling Model. In reality, this is contrary to the Socratic method, and the opposite of what Socrates described as wisdom. Knowledge itself isn't about having all of the right answers, but rather in knowing all the right questions to ask. Socrates said, "True wisdom is in knowing that you know nothing."

In my first book, My Judo Life, the main character, Cody Stephenson, has gotten laid off from his job, but had an appointment on the books to go to. He doesn't want to disappoint the person who had granted him time and he didn't have the phone number on his calendar that he left with, so he shows up. Once he is seated with the executive, the person asks Cody what he is selling. Cody replies with a very honest, "Nothing." This puzzles the executive and so he presses for clarification. Cody explains that he doesn't know what the person needs, so he has nothing to offer yet. Cody would not have normally sold in that manner, but he was in a very unique position. He really didn't have any product to offer. Cody began engaging the exec in conversation and uncovering what was actually important to the person and where he wanted to take his company. It was through the questioning, which Cody was simply using as a way to help, that the executive asked Cody for a full proposal to implement the ideas. Cody had not really intended to go into business, but he ended up in business because he had uncovered something of importance.

Too many salespeople in this world are going in with the idea of closing a prospect on a specific item that they sell. They are pushing their product instead of pulling direction from the prospect. It is only in making the needs of the prospect primary that they seek ways to meet our needs in business building. How many times have you had a sales rep, either by phone or in person, launch into their presentation without knowing anything about you? How many times have you thought to yourself, "This person doesn't care about me or my needs." If you are like me, virtually every telemarketer, almost every fundraiser, and a very large portion of direct sales groups come across this way.

One particular person, who was selling a supplement that would make me thinner, stronger, faster, better looking, able to leap tall buildings, etc., simply would not find out anything about me. After several minutes of her telling me how great her stuff was and how desperately I needed it, I asked her a couple of questions. I asked her, "What do you know about me?" and "What is it that you have seen in my life that would indicate I needed your product?" She was almost speechless for about 60 seconds. Finally, she started making assumptions about me and then told me that "Everyone needs this product!" While I think being passionate about what you offer is critical, it is in pushing that we repel others. Simple logic would tell you that if you push and push and push, eventually you reach the edge of the cliff for the prospect. When this happens, they "go off." I believe that it is this backwards model that has created so much fear related to the idea of selling. It shouldn't be this way and works better the other way.

Hypnotic Persuasion 101

The word, persuasion, comes from the 14th Century and it means… To induce someone to action. To induce means to pull as if magnetized in a direction. When we dissect the word, we discover that it never says to push, to force, to coerce, to cajole, or to close the person on doing something. It says that we are to pull the person in a specific direction and induce them to take action. We are to help them uncover the reasons that they have that would make it easy for them to decide to move forward. It is in their decided action that we find success. How often do we regret the decisions that we don't feel that we made? How often are we proud of the decisions that we know were ours?

If we make a decision to purchase something and it is wholly our decision, we tell our friends and associates. We feel justified in the decision. We are confident in our purchase. We are proud of what we know. We looked at what was important to us, evaluated our options, and chose a path to accomplishment. Buyer's remorse comes from people feeling duped into buying something. It is when a person felt pushed into action instead of pulled. I want you to take a moment and close your eyes and just try to remember a time when you were sold something that you regretted purchasing. How did you feel after that experience? How did it make you feel about the product, about the salesperson, about salespeople in general? Now, think about a time when you needed help figuring out what was right for you. Think about a person who served you by helping you discover the direction that made the most sense for your unique situation. When you decided on the purchase, that person facilitated the process and made it easy for you. It didn't feel as if they were selling anything. It felt as if they were there to assist you. You were open and honest with the person because you felt that they had your best interests at heart. That experience was drastically different than the other one.

It is the positioning of attitude that matters most. The attitude of discovery versus the attitude of mastery is what sets a truly great hypnotic persuader apart from a salesperson. If you walk into every sales situation with the following three components in place, you will walk out with someone who is loyal to you and focused on helping you find success. Please note that I did not say that you would always walk out with a signed agreement. I said that the person would be loyal to you and would help you find success. This means that people who don't buy will start marketing for you. The more people you have focused on helping you succeed, the easier success will be for you. So, here are the three attitudes of a hypnotic persuader.

1. I don't and can't know what the customer needs until I have had a conversation with them. Using a sales discovery model, like the one discussed in depth in the book, <u>Selling With Honor,</u> you can uncover the needs of the person. You will also be able to isolate their needs relative to the things that you offer. It is this isolation that makes it make sense in both a logical and an emotional state to purchase from you. Socrates taught that the key to unlocking knowledge was in knowing the right questions to ask. If you ask good questions, you get good answers. If you ask bad questions, you get bad answers. This means that you never ask the questions that put people on guard.

Instead, you ask the questions that help them see new information and make new decisions. An example would be, "Help me understand what is important to the success of your company. What would you say are 3 components of that success?" This creates a conversation. It is during the conversation that the person will reveal the critical decision factors that you need to understand. When they do share what is critical, you take note of it and anchor its importance. (You will learn anchoring in Chapter 7.)

2. People buy what is important to them and I will help them figure out what is important now. If a person begins to share with you what is important to them, dig deep into the "why" of that importance. It is in understanding their why that they will be open to your "how." When I first began my selling career, I would engage people in telling me why they did what they did, what frustrated them, what they were doing about it, and what they wish they could achieve but had not achieved yet. It was this conversation, which I had used in my non-profit days to raise money, that lead to them asking me how I could help. I didn't want to have to tell them what they needed to do. Like so many other people out there, I felt the idea of selling was scary. The idea of facilitating their

success through my tools and services, however, was very appealing. I always wanted to help with what was important. I found that people almost always wanted help with what was important as well. I have always wanted to be that helper. This sets me apart from almost everyone that I have competed with in the last 15 years. They were there to close a deal. I was there to facilitate the client's success, even if that meant that they should buy from someone besides me.

3. I don't want people to buy for the sake of a purchase. I want them to buy for the sake of their advancement and success. This would mean that your focus has to be on setting up buying opportunities and not on selling at all. I remember the first time that I told a prospect that it didn't sound like I had the product/service that they need, but I knew of someone that did. They furrowed their brow and pulled their head back slightly, as if to indicate confusion. I explained to them that it was my objective to ensure that they got what they needed and not just what I had to offer. I then coordinated the lady that I knew who had the right answer talking with the prospect. They had a great conversation and the prospect bought from my acquaintance. I didn't get a commission off of that. I didn't want

one. I wanted to help the person get what they needed, and that was it. That prospect never did buy from me. That was more than a decade ago and they have never given me a penny. They have, however, given me more than 20 referrals, most of which bought from me. I didn't do it for that reason, but I have made well over a quarter of a million dollars as a result of me not selling to them. In the end, they bought me because I cared more about them than the deal. That is a critical attitude to have.

Socrates taught that knowing that we know nothing is when true wisdom is gained. I have made it a point to read at least one book for personal development every month for over 15 years now. Every month, I feel as if there is so much more that I need to know. The more I learn, the more there seems to be out there to learn. Socrates also taught us that education is the spark that ignites the desire to learn. Education is not simply the transference of knowledge from one being to another. It is the use of knowledge transference to create a desire for more learning in the pupil. Who is the pupil, you ask? I am. You are. Anyone who desires to understand more in life, to achieve more in life, to create change in this world, to make a true difference, that is the pupil. If you walk into a situation with humility, others desire to learn from you. If you walk into a situation with arrogance, others desire to avoid you. Humility is the magnetic pull that you need with a client. Arrogance is the repelling side of magnets.

I would encourage you to buy a few magnets and play around with how the opposite polls of the magnet pull together and the like polls repel one another. When you are trying to be right, the prospect will try to be right and the two of you will repel each other. When you are trying to help them find success, then they are magnetically attracted to that same end result.

Pull! Don't Push!

6 LET'S FACE IT

When you are working with individuals and need to get a quick read for who they are and what the best methodology for communicating with them would be, using physiognomy is extremely effective. This is the science of facial structure as it relates to beliefs and thoughts. The face itself is a reflection of the thoughts and belief patterns of a person. At a glance, you can tell if a person is logical or emotional, relational or task oriented, and lots more. For the purposes of getting a quick read of a person, there are five (5) main areas that should be focused on related to the face.

Forehead – The forehead will be either flat across or rounded. This area of the face will indicate what the person needs in the way of information focus in order to process efficiently. For example, the flat across forehead (less rounded) requires facts, data, and logic. They need to hear the justification and need it backed up by what can be proven in order to believe you. In healthcare, this is the person that will want to see the chart or see the test results in order to buy in to what you are prescribing. The person with the rounded forehead needs emotional appeal in order to trust you. They are not looking for as much of the data as they are the connection. Typically, this person will require an additional 1 to 2 minutes of rapport building before they will be cooperative as a family member or patient. If you can keep in mind the best cognitive appeal (facts versus emotions) when engaging with a person initially, this will position you to gain their trust and their cooperation.

Eyebrows – The eyebrows will be in one of two primary shapes with the possibility of a spike or no spike in the hair of the eyebrows. The two primary shapes are rounded and flat. With each of these, there is the possibility of a spike on either or both sides of the brow. The flat eyebrows indicate a rational approach to people. This rational or logical approach to people means that the person will tend to engage for reasons that they can easily justify. In other words, they will have to see the benefit for themselves and the other person in order to enter into a relationship with them. The rounded eyebrows indicate a relational and emotional approach to people. These are the people that generally find it easier to engage with others. On the left hand side of the face, people will represent their beliefs about their personal lives. On the right-hand side of the face, people will represent their beliefs about their professional lives. It is possible to have a slightly different shape, as well as differed positioning of the eyebrows from one side of the face to the other. When a person has a spike in their left eyebrow (a place in the eyebrow hair that goes up from the rest of the brow in a spike or sharp arc), this indicates a need for control in their personal lives. It does not mean that they have control, just that they have a need for it. When a person has a spike in their right eyebrow, this indicates a need for control in their professional lives. If they have a spike on both sides, they just need control. ☺ The positioning of the eyebrow has meaning as well. The primary thing to look for is whether or not the eyebrow comes down just below the brow ridge. If it does, this indicates quick input-output. This is the person that often will say what is in their mind, even if they shouldn't. They have a weaker filter between their brain and mouth.

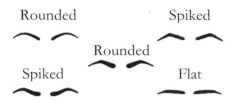

Rounded   Spiked

          Rounded

Spiked   Flat

Nose – There are two primary aspects of the nose to pay attention to. The first aspect is whether or not the person has a bump/ridge on their nose. The bridge of the nose will rise up, which represents the bump. This is the defensiveness bump. When a person has this on their nose, it indicates that they will "come out swinging" if they get backed into a corner. They are often very nice until they reach the point of being pushed too far. The second aspect on the nose is the lines on the sides of the nostrils. You could trace your finger from the lower corners of the nose (beside the face) up and around the sides of the nose toward the tip of the nose. The deeper those lines are, the more fiercely independent the person is. When a person is fiercely independent, they need choices, not instructions. For example, you would let them know that you needed their help to achieve a certain outcome and then ask them what the best process would be to get there. Another option would be to ask them whether they would rather choice A, choice B, or choice C and then let them decide which is best for them.

Chin – Just above the end of the chin, between the chin and the lower lip, will either be the presence of a line in an arch/half moon or the presence of smooth skin. When the line is present, this is known as the "verbal affirmation" line. It indicates that this person has a stronger need for appreciation when they do a good job or when they go above and beyond what is required of them. It is ideal to let them know what you appreciate about their specific behavior and how it has helped you. When this

43

person does not get the appreciation that they crave/need, they will often begin letting other people know that they are feeling undervalued. The second aspect of the chin that is relevant is the shape of the chin itself. It can be squared off / flat on the bottom, which indicates a strong focus on goals and achievement with a low tolerance for whining and complaining,. If this is the case, this person will be driven by and focused on achieving specific goals. They often come to work each day with a plan or a task list that they want and need to accomplish. The chin can be rounded, which indicates a focus on connection with people and the development of relationships. If this is the case, the person will approach work from the perspective of how they relate to others and what their relationships are like with others. Finally, the chin can come to a point. This is often a driven person, but they have become disillusioned with relationships. They are frustrated with being let down by others and don't feel that they can count on other people to do what they are supposed to do. Because of this, they are more prone to lashing out at others and making rash and aggressive responses to not having their needs met.

Ears – The final area to quickly read a person is their ears. The ears will be small and back towards the head, slightly larger and often sticking out more from the head, or will have a larger inner ear ridge than the outer ear cup. These three ear structures represent the learning and language patterns of the person. The ears that are smaller and closer to the head are the visual communicators and thinkers. They need visual words such as "picture this" and "I can see what you mean" or they need the use of comparisons in order to fully grasp a concept. You could say, "Doing this will be just like when we did that (description of another time). The larger ears that are often out away from the head represents the auditory thinker and learner. These types can hear and remember things very well. They often did well in public school because of the auditory nature of lectures and need words like, "think, process, dialogue, and listen." The final type of thinker and learner is represented by an ear that has a larger inner ear ridge than the outer one. This is the kinesthetic thinker/learner. This person processes information through action and intuition. Very often, you will see that nurses in a hospital setting are kinesthetic in their thoughts, while doctors are one of the other types, often auditory. This can pose a challenge, in that the doctors give instruction in their language pattern while the nurses need the instruction in their own. The kinesthetic thinker will use words like, "feel, my gut tells me, move, and act." If a person can tweak the words that they use, in order to stimulate the thoughts of the other person, the other person will be much better off and more able to understand. They will be connected to you almost instantly when you are speaking their language pattern.

Keep in mind that the quality of your communication is measured solely by the quality of the response that you get from others. If you are not getting a good response, you are responsible for changing your approach to that person or those people. I would encourage you to read this several times in order to get a full grasp of these five facial components. Consider the components in conjunction with one another in order to get the best read on another person.

Check out www.psycheofsuccess.com to take the "Faces of Reality" course to dive deep into understanding how to read anyone in 10 seconds or less. Also, checkout www.jodyholland.com for additional tools and resources on mastering this area.

7 DROP THE ANCHOR
RAISE THE SALES

Of course I realize that every self-respecting sailor would be raising their eyebrows at this point and wondering about the chapter title. After all, you don't raise the sails when the anchor is down. That would be counterintuitive when sailing the high seas. That's not what I said, though. I said to raise the "SALES," not the "sails." Think about what the purpose of an anchor is in sailing. It is to tether a vessel to a certain point. When a person drops their anchor from their boat, they are tethered to a certain point in the water. By the same token, when I say to drop an anchor, I mean to tether a person's subconscious to a certain point. Our objective here is to get people to focus on specific advantages of doing business with us, while keeping it their idea.

So, what type of anchors are there? Most anchors are verbal anchors, although there are also some that are physical. When we are anchoring a point, we are ensuring that a dominant focus that we desire becomes a dominant thought and belief that the other person has. This has to apply even after you are not with that person. The three main types of selling anchors that we will focus on in this chapter are Redirects, Future Thought, and Physical Anchors and Story Anchors.

Redirects

The redirect is the tactic of shifting the person's attention from the status quo to the desires for their success. One of the greatest challenges that we face in sales is in beating the status quo. What is happening right now is more of an enemy to success than the risks that a person might take. Let's say, for example, the person indicates that they are happy with what they currently have. We will want to say, "That's great. I am glad that you like what you have. What is it specifically that you like about your current product/service?" We give them the chance to talk about what they like and why they like it. We then ask, "If you could add even one thing to the solution that you have that would make your life better or easier or make your business more successful, what would it be?" We then listen to them talk about what is missing from the current solution. In a very conversational manner, we want to reiterate what they have said. For example, "You indicated that you like X,Y,Z about your current solution. You like the person that you do business with, but you said that it would be very nice to have A,B,C, which you don't currently get. Because that is important to you, and because you seem to be the kind of person who likes to move things forward, I would like to see if I can put together a package that has all of what you like in your current solution plus A,B,C that are important to you as well. May we get back together in a week to discuss the options to get you everything that you desire, including A,B,C?"

There are a couple of very important words that are trigger words to anchor this thought in their mind. The first word is the word "but." You have X,Y,Z, **BUT** you also want A,B,C. This language process will anchor in their mind that they are not, in fact, getting everything that they want from their current solution. The second trigger word is "because." In the example, I used it twice.

Because that is important to you, and **because** you seem to be the kind of person who likes to move things forward.

It is almost impossible for the person to argue with what they actually said was important to them, nor can they argue with the idea of being a person who moves things forward. The words, "moves things forward" is also planting in their mind the idea that things will be moving forward. By doing this, we are redirecting their dominant thought from the status quo to moving things forward. We use their own justifications to do so. It is not us coming up with a masterful presentation that they respond to or an "offer they can't refuse." It is us using their own words to anchor them in the right direction.

Future Thoughts

With this tactic, it is our objective to plant an idea in their mind that will come back to them at a later point in the day or in their life. People use this a lot more often than they may think. It is a very easy tactic that gets the person thinking about your ideas. As an example, you might say, "Later today, when you are interacting with your employees, and you are thinking about which ones of them are the best performers, I am sure you will be thinking about how great it would be to have more top performers just like them. Because you want great people, just like other successful leaders do, you will want to know what their internal makeup is. When that happens, I will be here to help and to map out that success pattern for you."

You are actually planting the thought of wanting to know what the internal makeup of their top performers is in their mind. You can do this with things that are positive and things that are negative. Another example would be, "If you are like other top leaders, you have been frustrated by the lack of performance of certain people. When this happens again, and it is likely to happen at least once in the next week, you will probably want to know what the difference is in the internal makeup of that person versus the top performer that you wish they were like. Because of this desire, we have created a tool that will do just that. When this happens in the next week, I am here to help you and to outline whether or not the non-performer has the capacity to perform at a higher level. I will leave the ball in your court, but I will be ready when you need me." The idea is to say these types of statements without coming across as arrogant or overly cocky. You want to be matter of fact and compassionate. It is ideal that you practice saying them in the mirror. Obviously, you will want to modify the statement to fit your industry and your specific focus area.

Physical Anchors

A physical anchor is something that we say that is connected to a specific touch. It is important that the touch is subtle and is in a location that is not offensive. This does not work if you are sitting across from the person. In fact, I think it would creep me out if you reached across and touched my elbow when we were sitting. However, this works great right before you are leaving. The touch only has to happen one or two times in order for the physical anchor to be in place. You can shake a person's hand as you are leaving, and then quickly reach out and pat/tap their elbow or shoulder and say, "I am here to make you more successful." This will appear to be a simple reassurance, but it will anchor the idea that you are the one that will make them more successful. The next time you see the person, you will want to reaffirm the same anchor. So that I remember what I have said and where I touched them, I really don't change my physical anchor from one person to another. I anchor the same idea into everyone's mind. My anchor is, "I am here to help." This anchor focuses on being altruistic (selfless and positive). It is an easy anchor for people to accept and it is how I am seen by lots of people that I work with.

By staying positive and focusing on doing good, it keeps me positioned in their mind as a helper and one that is of true value. Because of this, my invoices are paid when I send them. There are people who are seen as only out to help themselves that are in the same business that I am in. The difference is, I actually am there to help and I reinforce that often. You can even anchor thoughts in your own mind. My recommendation would be that you try the following...

Reach up and rub your left ear lobe with your left hand and say, "I am a motivated and happy person." I would recommend that you do this three times a day. When you do rub your left ear with your left hand and say that you are a motivated and happy person, you will see two interesting things happen.

1. You will begin to look for ways to be more motivated and happier.
2. You will start to crave your own positive reinforcement.

So, this evening, when you are looking in the mirror as you get ready for bed and thinking to yourself, "Is this guy crazy or is he a genius," you will feel the urge to reach up with your left hand and rub your left earlobe and say the reinforcement, just to see for yourself. After all, you only believe your own thoughts, not anyone else's thoughts.

Story Anchors

A story anchor is a command that is embedded

in a story. Zig Ziglar was a master of this anchor, using a story about someone getting over their hesitation to believe what Zig was teaching and becoming successful as a result of applying the information that he was sharing. He was embedding commands of what they were supposed to do and what they were supposed to believe without directly telling them to do so. By not telling them, but having a story about someone else telling Zig why it was important to do what Zig was saying, it was an excellent subconscious command!

Stories are actually very easy to use. I regularly use stories of client success, without naming the client, to explain what a person is going through and how, when someone just like them faced the same thing, I was able to work with them and help them find success. We are not threatened by the stories of other people facing struggles. We actually take comfort in knowing that we are not alone and that others have faced similar challenges. When a challenge is common and a technique has been used to solve the challenge before, even if it was with someone else, then it is easier to accept. This social proof, even if the prospect doesn't know the other client, is incredibly valuable.

Sales Away

Your objective is to find ways to use your anchoring skills to release the full potential of your sales. Think back to a time when you bought something from a person and truly enjoyed the experience, when you felt connected to them and felt that you could trust them. It was during that time, the one you enjoyed and appreciated, that the salesperson used these techniques. You will likely go about your business over the next couple of days and will think about those great buying experiences several times. It could be while you are cooking dinner, or while you are sitting and relaxing, however you relax, but you will have those moments where you wonder how you can create those same pleasurable buying experiences for others. As you ponder the idea of making buying fun and worthwhile for others, keep in mind that people respond well to anchors. My friend John said it best when he said, "I long for a time when I feel that spending my money is fun and fulfilling. It is so much more rewarding to know that I worked hard for something that was worthwhile. When a salesperson doesn't use these techniques, I am left wondering if they really even believed in what they were selling. Thanks Jody for helping me know how to create great experiences for my customers!"

That is my objective and I believe that it is yours as well. We all want our customers and guests to walk away knowing that they got what they wanted at a fair price. S0…

Drop Your Anchors and Raise Your Sales!

8 WORD UP

Each of us has a preferred language pattern. Some people prefer visual language. Others prefer auditory language. Still others will prefer kinesthetic language patterns. There are even two more, less used in business, language patterns that we use. Some people use gustatory and others olfactory patterns. The three main ones that we need to deal with are visual, auditory, and kinesthetic. Keep in mind that these are preferences. If your objective was to teach a course, you would blend each of the three primary styles into the way that you were presenting. If your objective is to open the eyes of your prospect, to move them to action, and to turn a great conversation into great action, then knowing these patterns is critical. They are critical because they are the preferences that your prospects will have. People tend to buy based on preference more that they do based on logic.

I want you to think back to a time that you really

connected with what was being said in a book, when you could see exactly where the author wanted to take you. Picture in your mind what you were thinking. What did you feel as you read the book? What did it make you want to do? If you were moved to action, inspired to performance, or even simply understood the process that the author was explaining, it was because you connected with their writing style. This means that they were writing in the style that resonated with you the best. People have a tendency to respond to language that is in their preferential style. The next three paragraphs are written in three separate language patterns, but say essentially the same thing. They are labeled for your reference. Read through them and see if you can feel the shift in language patterns from one to the next. Then, identify which paragraph resonated the best with you. This will help you to connect with your primary preference for learning.

Visual: Picture what it would be like to see yourself winning at every turn. You see your numbers growing everyday because of your application of the principles in this book. Once you have gone through the materials a few times, applying them will be like putting on your most comfortable pair of pants. People will have an image of you in their minds as the person that can solve their problems and make their life better because of the products and services that you provide. I know you can see it!

Auditory: Think about what it would be like to understand how to win at every turn. You have learned the system and your numbers are growing everyday because of your application of the principles in this book. Once you have gone through the materials a few times and have the sequence down, you will simply follow the process and achieve your results. When people think about you, they think... This is a guy that I can talk to and who will help me process through my challenges and think of the right answers. When you hear yourself speak, you simply know that the products and services that you provide are right for your customers. I know that you can hear them saying yes right now.

Kinesthetic: You are a person of action! As such, you charge forward and you win at every turn. You can feel success building in your life as your numbers grow daily. You don't just read the materials in this book, you apply them to the way in which you sell. You have a sense of understanding that gets stronger every time you sit down with a client. When your clients are near you, they get a sense of calm because they know that you are taking control of the situation and making the right things happen. The products and services that you provide are top notch and the satisfaction on your customers' faces proves it. You feel great about what you do because you inspire positive change.

This adaptation to the language structure that a person needs becomes very natural when you practice. In the beginning, however, it will feel as if you are working hard to speak in a new language. What has been so great is that people hear their primary language style first. This means that even though you may feel that you are struggling, and at times can't see yourself being successful at this, your prospect still connects at a deeper level with you than if you just used your own primary language patterns.

Mirror Mirror

Now that you understand that the other person's language pattern is important, here is the cool part. You can actually pull a person towards you. You will first need to mirror their patterns. You will need to use the same pattern as them, so that they can see that you are just like them, feel comfortable with you, and think that you are just like them. Once you do this for half a dozen sentences, you can start dropping in more of your own language style, which makes things flow more smoothly for you. The key is that you must reflect them first, and then they will reflect you naturally. You mirror, then they mirror. Almost nobody will even realize that they are adapting to meet your language needs.

This puts them slightly off balance and helps them to open up more toward you, and your ideas. Your objective should be to connect, then begin pulling them your direction. When you can begin to pull them toward your language, they will actually be giving up a layer of control. This means that they are becoming more and more willing to go along with what you suggest.

Now for the big hook… You will use your own language patterns, that they are now following, except when you anchor a thought. Like you learned in the chapter on anchoring, you will want to plant small suggestions with the way in which you structure your sentence (semantics). When you do this, match their natural pattern and then go back to your natural pattern. If yours is the same as theirs, you will still want to change yours, then switch back to theirs for the anchor.

The effective use of language patterns will create much more predictable results in your selling. If you are looking for success, want the feeling of success, and think that you are primed for it, use this technique on someone close to you. Try it out a few times on friends and family to see how incrediblye it works. The more you practice, the easier it becomes.

9 ASK AND YE SHALL RECEIVE

I remember sitting in an audience of more than 1,000 people when Zig Ziglar said that almost ¾ of all sales ended in failure for the same exact reason. As he said this, I moved myself forward a little in my seat, raised my chin and pointed my good ear toward the stage. I wanted to know why! I wanted to know why 72% of MY SALES were ending in failure. He then asked the question, "Do you want to know why?" I found myself shaking my head up and down and saying, "YES!" He said, "Well, I'm gonna tell ya'. The reason that most sales end in failure is because nobody asked for the business!" In his incredible Southern style, with a smile on his face, and with his right hand, thumb up, pointing toward me, and I swear it was right at me, he drove home the point. My sales were ending in failure, not because my products weren't good enough. They were ending without a purchase because I didn't ask. Steven Schiffman, author of more than 25 books on sales, once coached me on how to build my business faster by telling me,

"Jody, you have to stop confusing your potential clients by not asking for their business. You know that you are there to sell something. They know you are there to sell them something. Don't disappoint them!"

How many times have you gone into a presentation with the idea floating around in your head that you are NOT there to bring them on as a customer. Many people think that they don't want to be a pushy salesperson. Throughout this book, you have learned the keys to selling without coming across as "salesy". You have been learning that people love to buy stuff. You have even learned that they prefer to receive confirmation of their need to purchase from somewhere outside of their own head. Even knowing all of that, it is often difficult for people to put themselves outside of the situation and see what the variables are that change from being salesy versus being helpful. As I see it, there are really four (4) significant variations that move you from pushing people in a direction to leading people where they want to go. In order to make it easy to remember this, I have written it as an acronym. So, when you find yourself in the situation of trying to remember why you are there in front of the prospect, just remember D U D E! Because, dude, you are there to help!

> 1. <u>Desire</u>: You must have the desire to help. When you truly want to help and realize that you are there to help them move forward, then, and only then, will you focus on asking them to move forward.

It is your desire to make a difference that sets you apart from other sales people. Most sales reps go in thinking about making a quota, or pushing a certain product that is on special that month. You go in with a focus on what it is that they desire. You ask questions surrounding their needs, wants, actions, and outcomes. As you learned earlier in this program, you are there to figure out where they have been, what they are doing, and where they DESIRE to go next.

2. Understanding: In asking those questions, you are gaining an understanding of what they are currently doing and what outcomes those actions are producing. You are finding out how they see their situation. You are trying to see the world from their perspective. As such, you will be able to see what it is that you would want to do in order to move yourself forward. Without that understanding of their perspective, you will not be as prepared as you need to be in order to recommend the right actions, or the right pathway to success.

3. Dedication: This has to do with being dedicated to solving their problem/challenge even if you are uncomfortable at first. If your dedication is toward the resolution of their problem, then you will find them an answer, even if that answer isn't to use you and your

product or service. You will research what is going on with them, what others have done, and how to help them achieve their desired outcomes. The problem that many people have is that they are looking for a way to just plug in one option without knowing how that option can produce results. If you have qualified your prospect, then you shouldn't face this much. Your job is to desire to make their life better, understand what is keeping it from being better, and dedicate yourself to finding a solution for them.

4. Explanation: When you have explained their challenge back to them as you understand it, they will generally ask how you can help them overcome the challenge. It is at this point, that you should have a plan to get them where they want to be. You need to make sure that you are using their information to lead them to the "ask." If you have reviewed what they said, what they want, why they want it, and what you can do to help, then it is the time for action. The following are a few variations of asking for business.

- Based on what you have told me, it makes sense to move forward on this. I would like to have you as a client and help you solve this challenge. All I need is your autograph on this proposal to get started.

- Based on where you are and where you want to be, I believe that it is time for action. You indicated that you don't want to keep getting the same result that you have gotten in the past. You and I both know that it takes new action to get new results. I am ready to help you with that new action. If you can simply give me your autograph on this agreement, we can get started.

- I believe that you were right when you indicated that what you are doing now is not getting you the result that you want. I know that you want the very best for your business and I do, too. Let's work together to get you the results you are looking for. I just need you to sign here and I can get started helping you achieve new results.

The key is that you have to ask for what you want. You have to ask for their business. While it is true that there will still be people who don't choose to purchase from you, there will also be people who choose to purchase from you. More people will purchase if that is what you ask for than will if you don't ask for them to purchase. Knowing that it is a simple question that separates you from the success you desire, it makes sense to me to practice asking for what you want. I want you to do the following exercise as a practice in seeking what you desire.

The next time that you go to a restaurant, ask for something very specific from your waiter or waitress.

The next time you are asked what you want as a gift for any occasion, have something very specific in mind (within a reasonable budget) that you would like.

When you consider what you want from life, be very very very specific about what you desire.

Taking It Up A Notch

You said, because, you want, because, you need to move forward, because, and that's why. If you are a good listener, and really focus on what the prospect is saying, how they are saying it, and what they appear to be feeling when they say it, then you will be good at pulling out the right information in order to help solve their challenges. The word "because" is a very powerful word in hypnotic selling. It is the justification for action, the rationalization for change, and the catalyst for why things cannot remain the same right now. Let's break down what the sequence needs to be in order to inspire your prospect to buy from you as if they have always wanted to do just that.

You said: The focus needs to be very strong on what they said. The key to getting the information that you need is to ask the questions that lead only to that information. You will want to ask questions that center around what is important to the person. DO NOT ask obviously leading questions, such as, "Do you care about the future of your family?" That triggers the guards to go up in the conscious mind and makes it hard for the person to trust you. Instead, lay out some options of things that others find important, related to your industry, and ask them to choose which are the most important to them right now. In my business, we came up with the FIRSTEP model.

F.I.R.S.T.E.P. 2 Success Program
What's Important Now?

My team will slide a printed copy of this graphic in front of a prospect that we are visiting with and ask them which 3 are the most important to them. To date, we have not had a single person refuse to answer. The rep will then ask questions about each of the three areas that center around how they know that those are important to them. It feels very much like a conversation to the customer. By understanding what is important to them, we will have the answers to "you want" and "because."

Next, we will plant the suggestion that we should do something together in the next 60 days. We do this by saying, "If I had a magic wand and could fix one of those three areas for you in the next 60 days, which one would you choose?" It has always amazed me how quickly a person can choose the one that is most important to them. Next, I will ask, "Why is that one the most important?" I let them answer and I ask them good questions about their answer so as to probe deeper. After they have answered that, I ask them what they currently have in place to address their most important area. In reality, most people have used "HOPE" as a strategy instead of putting together an actual plan and solving their challenge. Hope is NOT a strategy. You will often find that they squirm a little because most people aren't doing anything to address what they have indicated is most important. Some will indicate that they are talking to you because they believe that it needs to be addressed. If they do have a process in place, which is rare, then ask them what they like about their current solution. Don't be that jerk that immediately starts telling people what is wrong with what they are doing. Instead, listen closely. The more you can match up your solution to the one they already thought was a good idea, the greater your advantage. Next, ask them what they wish that their solution provided that it doesn't currently. This the "gap" that they will want to fill with your solution. Some will only sell the gap. If you have been listening to the prospect, you will know how to replicate what they like from their current solution as well as fill in the gap, so that they have what they want completely. This dialogue gives you the answers to "you want" and "because."

Finally, I will ask why it would be important to

them to solve this challenge and make "what is most important to them" work the way that they want it to, see it working, and planned from the beginning. After asking "why it is important," I will expand on that by asking how it would benefit them to accomplish this and what it would be worth. After they discuss the benefits of making things better, I ask them what it will cost them to remain the same, or not fix it. By this point in the conversation, I have stirred up some strong emotions that are positive for a new direction and negative for the same old same old. This gives me the final component that I need, which is the "and that's why" in the formula.

Your opportunity to succeed rests in your willingness to ask for what you want in the right manner. If you will follow a formula similar to this one, you will find that people are eager to solve the challenges that are important to them and you no longer have to really "sell them" on using you. Your job becomes facilitating them buying what is right for them and their organization.

10 PEOPLE DON'T BELIEVE YOU

One of the simple truths that I learned early on in my selling career is that people don't believe you when you tell them what they need to do. They only believe what they told you to tell them back. They believe what they are saying, what their people are saying, and what the results are showing. So, you must understand how to not say anything and yet say everything that is necessary.

One of my great pet peeves is the telemarketer, or the sales rep, that uses lines like, "Do you care if your family lives or dies?" One such experience, which was actually from an in-person rep, was from a water company. They sell bottled water, rent the office dispensers, etc. Their water is actually very good and I would have been interested in buying from them, except... Well, here is the story.

Me: I am really interested in getting some water bottles custom labeled that I can use in my training programs.

Rep: That would be "x dollars for 20 cases."

Me: Wow! That is a lot more expensive than I was thinking.

Rep: Don't you care about your customers and what they drink?!

Me: No.

Rep: Well then, we can't help you.

What was so wrong with her approach was that she did not actually deal with my objection. She went straight to the guilt card. I grew up a preacher's kid and was exposed to guilt most of my life. It leaves a very bad taste in my mouth. Had she said, "When you say that it is very expensive, what are you comparing it to?" she would have gotten a much different response from me. I would have said, "Well, compared to the number that I had in my mind." I had not done any research on it, I just knew I liked their water and she was the first one that I talked to about it. She could have asked me what kind of budget I had for marketing and training supplies together, and then asked me what I was doing to remain relevant and to set a positive tone in the minds of my customers. I would have fumbled around and talked about doing a good job, branding everything, including the notepads, and trying to get them to see "me" everywhere. She could have then asked if people sipped on beverages throughout the day when I was training. I would have said yes and she could have asked what I was currently doing to ensure that everything I was doing was branded. I would have gone back to the other parts and made the connection that my water bottles really did need to be branded as well. I would have then started thinking about buying more than 20 cases to get my price down. She would have given me a few options with higher volume and we would have made a deal.

The challenge really wasn't the price. It almost never is. The challenge was that she was using what she thought should be my buying trigger instead of finding out what actually was my buying trigger. My trigger had almost nothing to do with what my customers thought about the water itself. Instead, it had to do with what they thought about my company and knowing that those water bottles would be a constant branding reminder of how I was helping to make their lives better in every way. Chances are, I would have bragged about the added minerals in the water which would boost cerebral function and increase retention. This correlation would be one more reminder why my business was the one that they had chosen.

When we sell on our own preconceived notions, we often miss the boat. We need to stop selling and start creating buying opportunities. Think about it! I love to buy stuff! You probably love to buy stuff as well. Most people really enjoy buying, but very few people want to be sold. Buyer's remorse comes from being sold something that you weren't actually ready to own. People who are convincing you to let them buy something don't usually have remorse. After all, it was their idea, at least in their mind it was, that is.

Too many sales reps go into a sales setting with the five-step model of selling...

1. Establish the greatness of the company that you represent.
2. Identify their pain.
3. Intensify their pain.
4. Explain how your product/service is the only thing that can fix it.
5. Explain how what they are doing isn't, won't, and can't work, unless you come in and save the day.

I don't know about you, but I get pretty upset at the idea that I was "rooked" into buying. I don't ever want to feel like I was sold, taken advantage of, or tricked into something that was not right for me. Because of that, I would offer the following.

1. Identify what is important to the prospect.
2. Learn about why it is important to them.
3. Learn about what they are doing to put focus on that.
4. Discuss with them what they like about their current solution and what is missing.
5. Fill in the gap of what is missing with your product.

If it is their idea to buy from you, they will be proud of the purchase and will tell their friends, and even post about it on social media. If it was your idea, your words, they will struggle with justifying it at all. People believe everything that they believe. If it is a thought that originates in their head, then they claim it. Thoughts are the byproduct of hypnotic suggestions, all…day…long.

Everywhere you turn, there are subliminal suggestions designed to draw the right thoughts out of you. With this model of hypnotic selling, persuasion is significantly intensified. You become the savior for your prospects because they have always been looking for a way to fill the gap, solve their challenge, and focus on what is important to them. They already believe their own thoughts. They already want an answer. You are simply the person who cares about identifying the place where the answer goes.

People will not believe a salesperson. They have been conditioned not to. They will, however, believe their own thoughts, even if you were the catalyst for those thoughts. Your capacity to help people realize their objectives is incredible. It is incredible because you now possess the tools to move your clients forward and upward toward success. You now know what it means to be hypnotically persuasive.

This is some powerful information that you now possess. It is like having the key to a kingdom of riches that never runs out. Imagine how it feels to help your customer reach their fullest potential. The more successful they become, the more they will want to do business with you. The more you help other persuaders learn these goals, the more they will help other individuals and companies succeed. You are primed to be a positive catalyst, if that is what you choose to do.

It is up to you to determine how you use this

information. It was my intention to equip you with the tools to be a superstar salesperson. It was, and always will be, my hope that you will use this newfound power for good, and for the growth of your company and your clients. Now, what is it that you desire for this world? Do you desire that others learn, grow, and prosper? I would encourage you to write out in 3 sentences or less exactly what you hope that others will accomplish as a result of what you now know. If you choose to share this book, please make sure that you share it with people who have a strong desire to make the world a better place, like you.

I wish you all the success in the world!

Jody N Holland

ABOUT THE AUTHOR

Jody Holland is an author, speaker, trainer, online course creator, business coach and entrepreneur. He has started several successful companies and focuses on bringing out the best in others. Jody has written 20 books and dozens of training programs, which can be found on Amazon.com and JodyHolland.com respectively. He is married with two cool kids and lives in Texas with his family. Check out www.jodyholland.com, www.psycheofsuccess.com, and www.amazon.com/author/jodyholland

Made in the USA
Monee, IL
02 December 2021

82928227R00046